WALL STREET LIES

WALL STREET LIES

5 Myths to Keep Your *Cash* in Their *Game*

TED OAKLEY, PAT SWANSON,
AND TREY CRAIN

Copyright © 2016 by J. Ted Oakely, Pat Swanson, Trey Crain

All rights reserved. No part of this book may be used or reproduced in any manner whatsoever without prior written consent of the author, except as provided by the United States of America copyright law.

Published by Advantage, Charleston, South Carolina.
Member of Advantage Media Group.

ADVANTAGE is a registered trademark and the Advantage colophon is a trademark of Advantage Media Group, Inc.

Printed in the United States of America.

ISBN: 978-1-59932-751-8
LCCN: 2016945691

Cover design by Katie Biondo.

This publication is designed to provide accurate and authoritative information in regard to the subject matter covered. It is sold with the understanding that the publisher is not engaged in rendering legal, accounting, or other professional services. If legal advice or other expert assistance is required, the services of a competent professional person should be sought.

 Advantage Media Group is proud to be a part of the Tree Neutral® program. Tree Neutral offsets the number of trees consumed in the production and printing of this book by taking proactive steps such as planting trees in direct proportion to the number of trees used to print books. To learn more about Tree Neutral, please visit **www.treeneutral.com**.

Advantage Media Group is a publisher of business, self-improvement, and professional development books. We help entrepreneurs, business leaders, and professionals share their Stories, Passion, and Knowledge to help others Learn & Grow. Do you have a manuscript or book idea that you would like us to consider for publishing? Please visit **advantagefamily.com** or call **1.866.775.1696**.

TABLE OF CONTENTS

1 | INTRODUCTION
Do You Trust Wall Street? Should You?

7 | LIE #1
A Wall Street Broker Is a Reliable Investment Manager

13 | LIE #2
The Stock Market Always Goes Up

21 | LIE #3
The Bigger the Financial Institution, the Greater Your Investment Options

27 | LIE #4
Wall Street Has Your Best Interest in Mind

35 | LIE #5
The Wall Street Model Is Investing's Gold Standard

41 | CONCLUSION

45 | ABOUT THE AUTHORS

INTRODUCTION

DO YOU TRUST WALL STREET? SHOULD YOU?

Working on Wall Street in the late 1970s gave me a chance to see firsthand how things worked in the investment center of the world. It was a disillusioning experience—a close-up view of a business model that was at times rife with corruption, greed, and disregard for the sanctity of the obligations financial advisors should have to their investors. It was a world that was often filled with lies, and it still is today.

Four decades later and 1,600 miles removed at my Oxbow Advisors investment management company in Texas, I know the manipulative antics I witnessed on Wall Street long ago were just a warm-up for the massive deceptions that were yet to come. Consider the doomed computer lease investments of the 1970s, real estate tax shelters of the 1980s, all the money funneled into the Japanese stock market in the early 1990s, and then, at the bottom of the barrel, the overrated and oversold mortgage-based securities of the mid- and late-2000s that eventually led to the erasure of over $4 trillion in global wealth.

No matter what big, corporate-motivated moves the giant Wall Street investment firms make, there are always implications for financially prudent companies like mine. Over the years, my managers have spent a great deal of time defending and protecting investors from the continual onslaught of Wall Street sales ideas. We've opened many eyes to predatory tactics and get-rich-quick scams. We've also helped financially wounded investors clean up the damage after their affiliations with Wall Street went sour—finding ways to salvage the wealth they still possessed.

Like the majority of my investors, I built my business by working diligently, building honest relationships, and making prudent decisions. If you are a business owner or have recently sold your business, I'm betting you created your success and accumulated your wealth the same way. But that's not the way Wall Street works. Rather than focusing on wisdom and work, it inevitably prioritizes the quick dollar over the hard-earned one.

On some level, I think most investors know this truth, and yet the temptation to be drawn in by the size, scope, and sales prowess of Wall Street firms is still strong. At Oxbow, our managers have asked countless business owners and former business owners this one simple question, "Do you trust Wall Street?" Overwhelmingly, the answer is not just "no" but "not at all." But despite that intuitive suspicion from hard-working entrepreneurs, the Wall Street machine still generates and perpetuates a lot of investment myths that have taken hold in our society, and it continues to draw in investors who should know better but don't.

As a business owner or former business owner who sold a company, you will find that the majority of Wall Street views the concept of risk much differently than you do. You perceive it as the likelihood of not reaching your goals—or, worse, as suffering the loss of a large part or all of your capital. You aspire to maintain purchasing power over the life of your investments. You have enough capital to last a lifetime, and your priority is to maintain and grow that capital. With those goals, you don't have to "beat the market" to succeed. Wall Street sees things differently, focusing on a get-rich-quick mentality, excessive exposure to risk, and corporate profit above all.

This book is designed to alert you to the five biggest Wall Street lies and to demonstrate how dangerously wrong they are. In the chapters that follow, you'll learn why a broker by any name is not the most trusted steward of investor wealth. You'll learn why it's foolish to trust in the stock market always going up. You'll see that a bigger financial institution does not always offer the most or best investment options. You'll find proof that the big-name brokerage firms do not have your best interests in mind as they try to steer your investment choices. And you'll learn how the Wall Street investment model systemically favors its own shareholders' interest over that of its investors.

If your gut tells you that you can't trust Wall Street, you're right. As it has grown increasingly, unimaginably vast and powerful, it's become bigger than the ethics, experience, or accountability of any one individual who is part of it. This book is designed to even the playing field a little by showing the flip side of the myths the brokerage industry imposes on investors every day. We hope you enjoy reading *Wall Street Lies*.

—*Ted Oakley, founder and managing partner, Oxbow Advisors*

LIE #1

A WALL STREET BROKER IS A RELIABLE INVESTMENT MANAGER

The myth of the reliable broker may be the biggest Wall Street lie of all, and every investor needs to know why this statement is patently false. There is a fundamental difference between what a Wall Street broker does for a living and what a credentialed investment manager does—and that difference lies in the essential nature of how each group makes money. It boils down to this: investment managers get paid for what they do; brokers get paid for what they sell.

Over the years, a lot of Wall Street firms have manipulated broker titles to blur the lines between these two very different functions, using names like "wealth manager" or "investment team" to imply a high level of fiduciary responsibility. That's a good way to confuse the public—and to perpetuate the idea that Wall Street brokers are first and foremost concerned with protecting and growing their investors' wealth. Regardless of their titles, though, any investment professional who is not managing money for a fee is not doing it out of the kindness of his or her heart. That person is a broker who sells product—frequently proprietary or even high-risk product—for profit. When investors blindly entrust those brokers with their hard-earned fortunes—misguidedly believing they're under the wing of a trusted advisor—that makes it all the easier for the broker to sell, sell, sell his or her product of choice with little or no resistance.

On the other side of the wealth management coin, Registered Investment Advisors, like the members of my investment committee at Oxbow, are fee-only professionals who are paid to manage money, not to sell products for our own benefit. Because of that distinction, our first and most important accountability is to our investors. If we don't provide them with intelligent, sound guidance, they don't stick around. Does that mean the investments we choose always win? Of course not. That's not the nature of the industry. Investing always involves risk. But it does mean that we do all our homework, thoroughly research our investments, study historical data, and keep our eyes on the long-term benefits. Every choice we recommend to or make on behalf of our investors is based on preserving and growing their wealth. No Wall Street investment firm can honestly make that statement—that's not the way their system works.

How does our process differ from the way Wall Street's brokerage firms look out for their investors' best interests? Here's a stunning statistic to consider. Just since 2009, big Wall Street institutions have accumulated over $200 billion in fines for questionable practices. Only the Wall Street machine—so powerful it seems impervious to even the most scathing indictment of its flaws—could continue to function and pull in new investors with a record like that. Through it all, these institutions miraculously perpetuate the myth that they are the best stewards of investor funds.

We're money managers. They're salespeople getting paid on commission. They can wear a fiduciary hat when it suits them, but in order to succeed, they must wear the sales hat. They are never "fee-only." Sometimes they're "fee-based," but that's another label that helps hide sales as their primary interest. These professionals do everything they can to obscure the lines between financial-advising professionals and broker-dealers, and they're good at it.

As a wise businessperson and investor, you should weigh your choice in investment advisors just the way you'd approach any important decision in your business—considering all candidates on the basis of qualification and experience, accountability, track record of success, and alignment with your values and priorities. Many Wall Street investment houses offer the illusion of all these things, but the reality can be starkly different: inexperienced brokers hiding behind their big-name employers; individuals several places removed from the decision maker for your assets having low accountability for the products they sell; people who are part of an industry where the name of the game is creating a return for shareholders no matter what—even if that means saddling trusting investors with subpar products to make it happen.

Think about it this way. As a business owner, you would never dream of entrusting the fate of $5 million, $10 million, or $100 million in assets to someone you'd only known for a few weeks, someone with a questionable track record, or someone whose priorities for your assets do not align with yours. But in the world of investing, people do it all the time, handing over tens of millions of dollars to brokers with the clout of major Wall Street investment banks tied to their names.

FIVE QUESTIONS TO ASK

If you own a business—and especially if you've recently sold a business—chances are you're getting calls every day from Wall Street "experts" who want to invest your money. Before you make any decisions, take the time to answer these five questions:

1. How does the financial advisor get paid? Is compensation based on sales success or on responsible management of your assets?

2. How does the financial advisor intend to understand your unique priorities and make investments that are in line with them?

3. How will you communicate with the decision maker for your investments? In other words, are you speaking with the person who will be the steward of your money—or is that person two, three, or more degrees removed from your contact?

4. How does this financial advisor plan to both protect and grow your investment capital to ensure that you never lose the security you now have to live out your life on the strength of your current assets?

5. How is this financial advisor—not the company he or she works for but the individual—uniquely qualified to be entrusted with your life's savings?

By the time you're through getting answers to these questions, you should have a good idea of whether you're talking with a reliable investment manager or a Wall Street broker posing as one. That should make it much easier to see beyond the myth of the reliable broker so you can make an informed, intelligent decision about whom to trust with your hard-earned investment dollars.

LIE #2

THE STOCK MARKET ALWAYS GOES UP

The myth that the stock market always goes up is one of the most popular and overused adages about investing in public securities. While this statement may hold true in the extreme long run, there is a lot more to your financial future than just a hundred-year stock market chart. Every individual has a different investment objective and investment period, and relying on a stock market going up eventually isn't much of a security blanket—especially since it may in fact not go up during the investment period that matters to you.

The first problem with the cliché of the ever-rising market is there are inevitably periods of slow and stagnant growth—or even no growth at all—in any economy. Even the heartiest and wealthiest have them. These conditions can cause downturns and sideways movement in the markets. When these periods occur and you need to pull cash flow or money from your accounts, that can be detrimental to the overall performance of your assets.

If you look at the following chart, you'll notice that since 1915 there have been several significant periods of sideways movement. From roughly 1965 to 1983 there was a stretch of almost seventeen years of no rise in the stock market. From 1999 to 2013 there was also a long period of little to no growth. For investors, periods like these are extremely frustrating, especially when they see multiple declines of -25 percent to -50 percent in a portfolio. If you are one of the unfortunate investors who ends up waiting on an aggressive market investment for more than a decade without seeing any growth, you'll find very little consolation in the idea that the stock market always goes up. *Always* doesn't mean every year or even every decade—it just means someday.

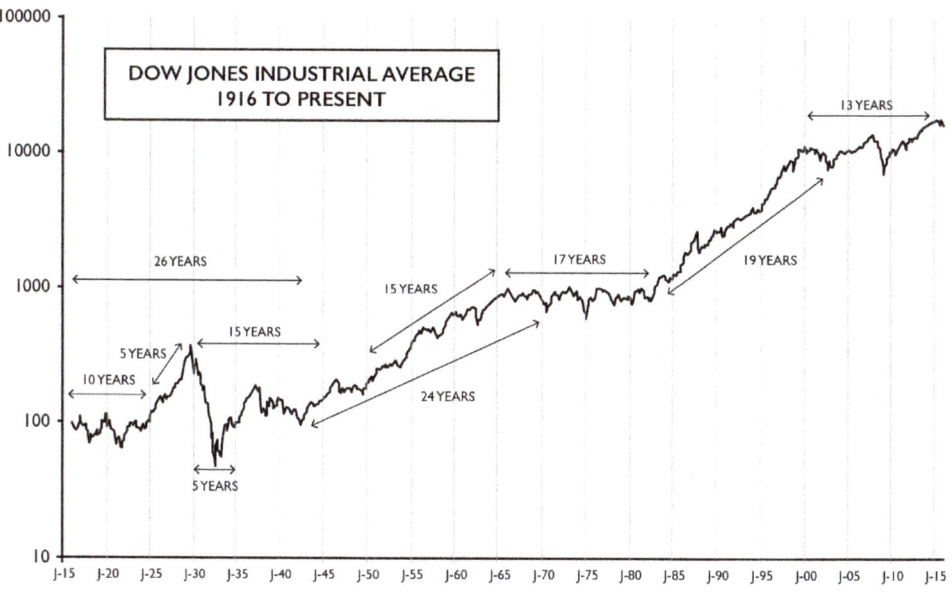

In the graph above, note the long periods of stagnant and net-even markets. The stock market may always go up in the long term, but that's no consolation for investors who needed to see returns during these sometimes decade-long droughts. (Source: Oxbow Advisors)

Each investment period is different, but you have to maintain a steady cash flow and invest in high-quality companies to make it through volatile times. Whether you have stocks, bonds, real estate, or private investments, you have to know what you own and what kind of cash flow you can expect. It can become increasingly frustrating to chase the stock market, trusting that it will always go up—only to end up exactly where you started fifteen years on.

You can see another powerful example of this when comparing the cumulative market return from 1928–1954 with that of 1954–1965. From 1928 to 1954, the cumulative return, or the total return, was 1.69 percent, representing essentially twenty-six years of totally stagnant markets. That could easily be an individual's entire retirement life, and he or she could end up losing a significant amount of money if principal was not protected in the early years. The latter part of the comparison, 1954–1965, saw a roughly 154 percent return over eleven years, which is a tremendous return. However, those who were unable to protect themselves from the downslide in the previous years missed out on this significant capital appreciation. For them, retirement undoubtedly looked a lot different than for those who came to the market later.

This brings us to the second related problem with the cliché of the stock market always going up: a failure to focus on investment start date. You'll almost never hear of an advisor from a Wall Street firm bringing this to an investor's attention. Most of their advisors and money management firms are eager to invest your money all at once in the markets or in their asset allocation models. Because of the myth of the markets always going up, they don't necessarily care about, or even consider, the investment starting point. But when you consider an initial investment into the public markets, your starting point is one of the biggest factors in your long-term portfolio success—or failure. The fact is, if you face a decline in the first three years, the impact can be devastating. If you face a decline in the last three years, your assets may be reduced, but the impact will be less damaging.

Take a look at the following chart to see how this important distinction plays out. Each of these investors starts out with $5,000,000 in a portfolio. Michelle's portfolio has steady growth of 9.5 percent in the early years and then a -15 percent decline each year for three years. Ryan, on the other hand, *starts* with a -15 percent decline each year for three years. These investors are assumed to be taking out $250,000 (5 percent) the first year and increasing their withdrawals 2 percent every year thereafter to keep up with inflation. Because of his early losses, Ryan eventually depletes his portfolio, ending up with nothing. Michelle, who started with the same initial portfolio, winds up with her initial investment still intact, plus a substantial return. Each of these portfolios went through years of market growth and years of decline, but the determining factor in their outcomes was simply which investor timed entry into the markets better than the other.

There's a good chance that Ryan, who ends at $0, was told throughout the duration of his investments that *the stock market always goes up* and advised that his fortune would change in a downturn. His is a perfect example of this fundamental problem with most brokerage firms and their investment advisors: they do not stress enough that the starting period is the most important twelve to twenty-four months of an investment.

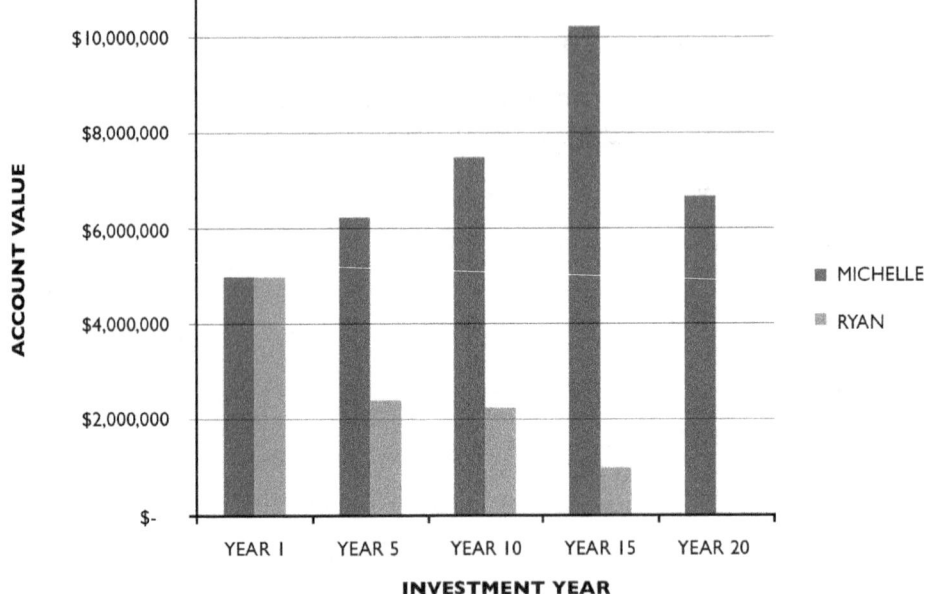

The graph above illustrates two hypothetical investors. Each withdraws $250,000 in the first year and increases withdrawal by 2 percent every year after. Ryan's investments suffer losses in their first three years; Michelle's suffer losses in their last three years. The starting point for these portfolios is the single biggest determining factor of their very different outcomes.
(Source: Oxbow Advisors)

The financial markets can be confusing and overwhelming, which makes it easy for investors to believe it when they're told the markets always go up. In truth, there should be a lot more to any individual's financial plan than jumping into the markets with both feet and a high percentage of his or her assets. Look at your situation in detail. Always remember that, at some point during your investment period, protection of principal will be more important than investment growth—and it's hard to do that when your risk tolerance is overextended.

LIE #3

THE BIGGER THE FINANCIAL INSTITUTION, THE GREATER YOUR INVESTMENT OPTIONS

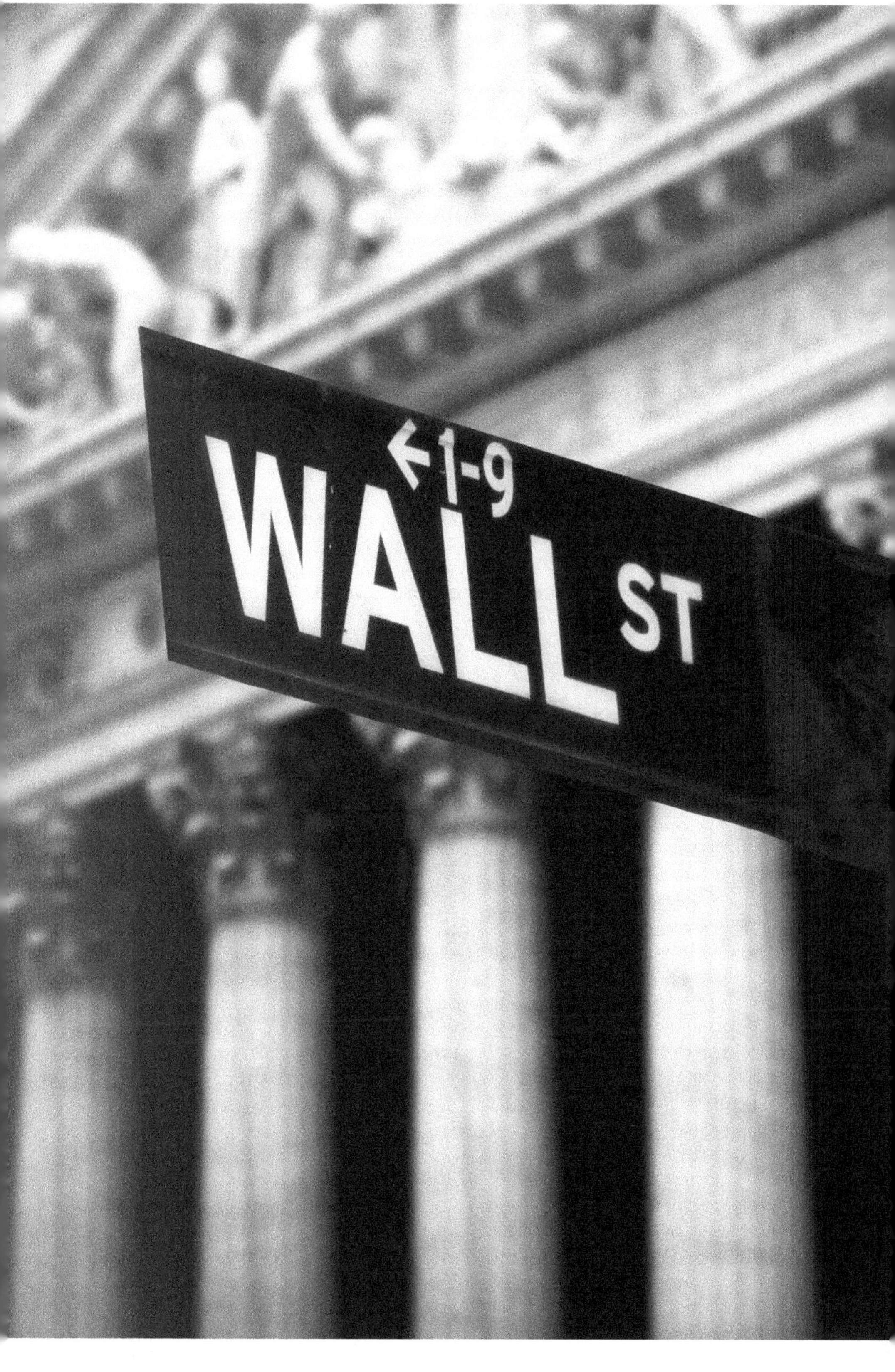

1-9
WALL ST

We all know the brand name investment firms. How could we not? Their advertisements and pitches are everywhere, and if you're a business owner or someone who's recently sold a business, they've probably reached out to personally connect with you, to tell you all they have to offer. They'd like you to think that by investing with their financial institutions, wirehouses, and banks, your money will not only be secure but effectively and efficiently managed. Their slogans say it all, heavy with references to *confidence, protection, strength, vision, loyalty, and growth.*

Since they boast hundreds of billions in assets under management and tens of thousands of wealthy clients across the globe, it's easy to believe without questioning that these largest players on Wall Street must provide the most diverse options for managing your money. It's easy to believe, but it's not true. The reality, as we all witnessed in the 2008 banking crash, is that many of these large, seemingly rock-solid investment firms are anything but stable. This couldn't have been more apparent during the '08 financial crisis when several notable investment banks sold highly profitable securities to their clients—while simultaneously betting *against* those same investments. These large financial institutions kept their shareholders and stock prices squarely in focus—all eyes on making money for the house—but simply failed to manage the broader risks.

As a rule, Wall Street's priorities in guiding investors are murky. Despite the sophisticated sales pitches of its agents, the options it offers its investors are most often those that are best for its own accounts, its shareholders' returns, and its corporate bottom lines. Since these institutions must support their large advertising budgets, marketing departments, endless overhead, and the myriad expenses associated with operating thousands of branches and offices, this should come as no surprise. Nevertheless, their limitations are often repackaged and redelivered to investors in a way that masks their deficiencies.

With tens of thousands of registered representatives on salary, big Wall Street banks cannot guarantee each employee will adequately explain the features, benefits, and risks of varying and sophisticated strategies and investments. That complexity and potential for variance between client portfolios creates a lot of liability for them. As a result, their "advisors" are largely relationship managers, far removed from the actual decision-making process. The real decisions about where client investment dollars go are made by a smaller pool of professionals who have no direct contact with, or in most cases, knowledge of, the people behind the money. This is in sharp contrast to a small investor-focused company like Oxbow, where our partners believe understanding our investors' priorities and being directly accessible to them are essential parts of our roles as steadfast, forward-looking advisors.

Another way most Wall Street firms fail to make all the appropriate investment options available is surprisingly simple: these large institutions routinely limit their risk by limiting what they sell. They offer a family of funds and investment products marketed by their sales teams and run by their portfolio managers (none of whom you will likely ever meet). Armed with only a rudimentary understanding of your situation and needs, the relationship manager constructs your optimal portfolio from this limited menu of funds and products, all the while keying in on buzzwords like "asset allocation" and "portfolio rebalancing." Despite the fact that the salesperson may cheer your newfound investment diversity, chances are, if you look closely, you'll find you're still placing all of your eggs in one basket.

At the end of the day, most Wall Street managers, executives, and even shareholders want you to purchase the most profitable products and investments . . . for the institution's bottom line. So when the relationship manager suggests products and vehicles run by his or her employer, your keen business sense should sound an alarm. Why are you being pushed to buy these particular products or being limited to a particular family of funds? Is the "advisor" compensated by your portfolio's performance or his or her performance in meeting sales quotas? These are just some of the questions you should ask when determining if the advice you're receiving is free of conflict and in your best interest.

From high and often hidden fees to low performance, Wall Street's proprietary platforms and practices deserve careful scrutiny. You don't have to take any one advisor's word for it—public record is chock-full of examples of high-profile banks steering their clients into expensive proprietary funds over those of other families.

Wall Street is full of smart people, and its executives have long recognized these shortcomings in their investment options. In order to avoid scrutiny and retain more clients, some brokerage houses have added investment options offered by other institutions and companies. This sounds like a viable solution, and at first glance, the prospect seems unbridled and free from conflict. But on closer inspection, these alternatives are often shrewdly limited. Worse, their availability on the menu has just as much to do with the institution's bottom line as your investment returns. Behind the scenes, third parties are quietly paying these institutions for the privilege of being on their platforms. In addition, the institutions incur expenses in sourcing and negotiating their external fund managers. These expenses are ultimately passed on to the client through layers of fees.

While you may be more diversified from a manager perspective when you buy into these options, once you do, there are more mouths to feed from your investment returns. The entire scheme is usually just a way for Wall Street to repackage another one of its limitations.

By contrast to the Wall Street investment option model, truly independent managers aren't confined to one family of investments, funds, or asset classes. We are owned by the partners themselves—not shareholders—and we answer only to our investors. Truly independent advisors have the ability to offer their investors more in the way of investment options *because* of our independence, not despite it.

LIE #4

WALL STREET HAS YOUR BEST INTEREST IN MIND

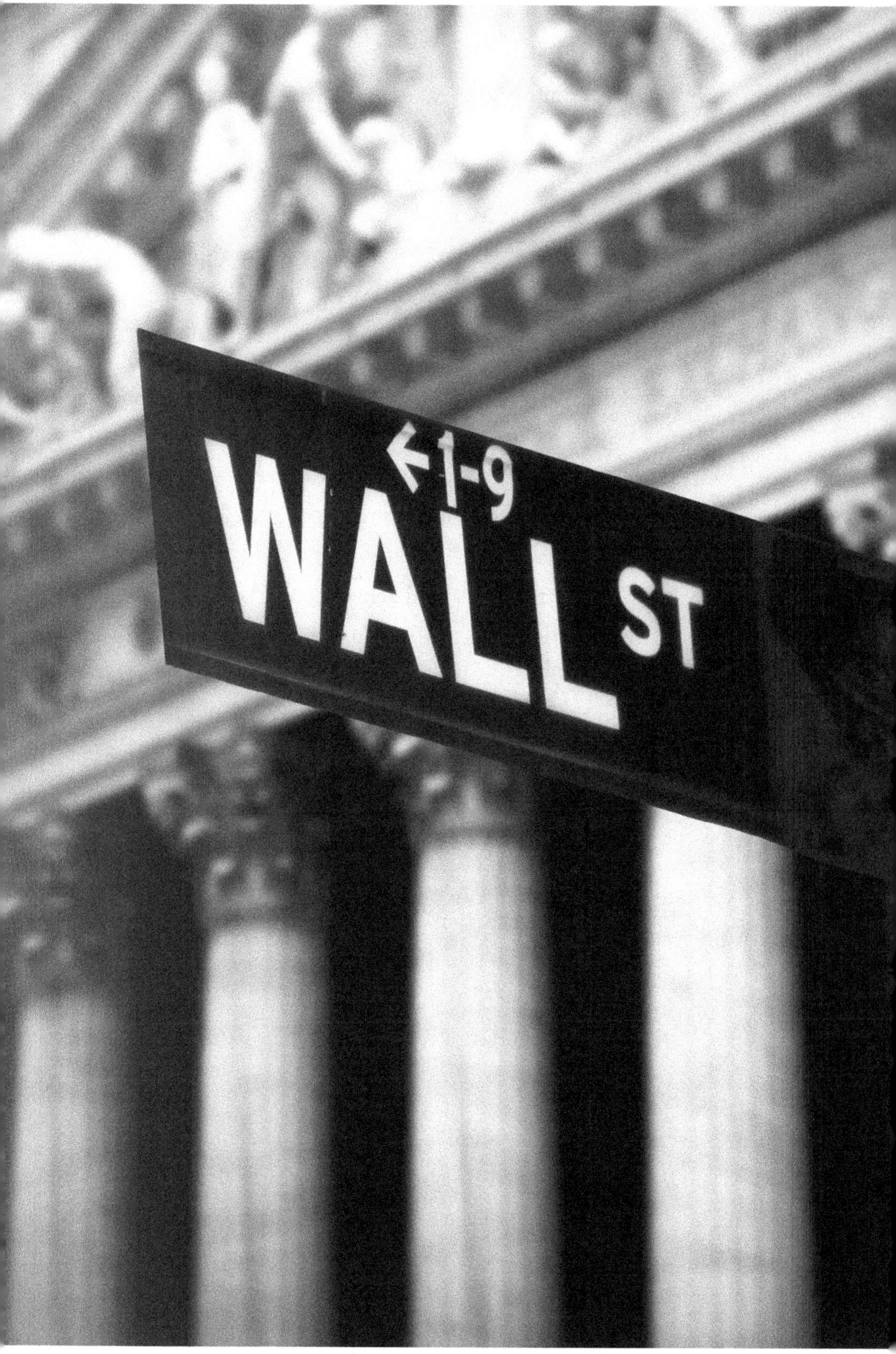
←1-9
WALL ST

For some, there's a comfort level that comes with investing through an institution that's been dubbed *too big to fail*. Placing your life's savings under the wing of a Wall Street investment house, with all the size and clout their names imply, may feel like a safe bet. The big-name brokerage houses certainly want you to think they can be counted on, that they have your best interest in mind, but that's yet another Wall Street lie. The fact is, Wall Street stacks the deck every day and in every facet of its dealings to protect its own interests—not that of its investors.

On some level, we already know this. In recent decades, the image of Wall Street has come to be more closely associated with the dark side of American capital markets than with the security and stability it once represented. This shift acknowledges the self-dealing, short-sightedness, overleveraging, and dangerous herd mentality of today's Wall Street. These institutions, run by obscenely powerful broker-dealers and banks, have tremendous influence on our financial system. But they are not wielding that power and influence on behalf of their investors. Instead, they operate on systems that are rife with internal conflicts of interest.

Consider these main reasons Wall Street is failing to protect your interests.

WALL STREET IGNORES MARKET FACTS

Wall Street and the financial press frequently rely on simplistic historic averages to project future returns. How many times have you heard you should invest most of your nest egg in stocks since equities, including dividends, have returned an average of 11 percent annually since World War II? That advice is everywhere on Wall Street, but as we discussed in chapter 2, the problem with those averages and other statistics like them is they don't tell you much.

While it's true the S&P 500 returned 10.7 percent *on average* from 1945 to 2015, the *range* of returns during that seventy-year period is immense, bounded by the worst year (-36.5 percent) in 2008 and the best year (51.2 percent) in 1954. Surprisingly, there are only three years in the seventy that have a return that's close to the overall average: 11.6 percent in 1959, 10.8 percent in 1968, and 10.7 percent in 2004. The fact is, earning an average return in a given year is *not* a given; it's a rarity.

WALL STREET ALWAYS LOOKS BACKWARD

Most often, Wall Street brokers navigate by looking through the rearview mirror, basing their asset allocations on past returns. In doing so, they often fail to consider market conditions with a client's new cash. In particular, they disregard the need for larger cash reserves when market valuations are high. Consider today's overvalued bond market. We're approaching the end of a thirty-five-year bull market in bonds; since late 1981, ten-year US Treasuries have fallen from 15.8 percent to 1.8 percent. At such low levels, the prices of bonds are extremely sensitive to changes in long-term interest rates. In fact, as an example, a twenty-five-year US Treasury bond will drop 12 percent for only a single percentage point increase in rates! How will Wall Street react when interest rates go up two or three percentage points? There's no way to know, because today's trading desks and strategy teams are full of a generation of brokers who have never seen how higher interest rates impact their markets.

What we do know—what we see time and again as we try to help investors recover from financially damaging interactions with Wall Street—is that it's only the rare Wall Street broker who will warn you of the high risks of any investment choice. Instead, most have remarkably short memories and choose to disregard the stunning -32 percent stock market loss in just two months of 1987, the -50 percent loss from September 2000 to March 2003 as the Internet bubble burst, and the -57 percent loss from October 2007 to March 2009.

WALL STREET PUSHES PROPRIETARY PRODUCTS AND RISKY ALTERNATIVE INVESTMENTS

While many Wall Street-associated investment teams declare they are "open-architecture"—able to use investment strategies and experts not associated with their firms—this is seldom the case. Ask any Wall Street broker to purchase a security that is not a proprietary product of his or her firm. More often than not, the broker will balk, explaining that compliance issues prevent the purchase. Most likely, the broker will offer you an "equivalent" in-house strategy—one where the team gets a bigger slice of the fees.

Another fascination of Wall Street is alternative assets, particularly hedge funds and private equity investments. Both are usually private, limited partnerships that generate bountiful fees for their managers and Wall Street brokers. The question is, *do these favorite schemes of big-named firms serve investors' interests?* In many cases, the answer is a resounding *no*.

Hedge funds are sometimes referred to as "compensation schemes" rather than an asset class—and for good reason. For starters, their typical fees are 2 percent annually plus 20 percent of profits. That's a very big cut for the manager/advisor. As long as returns are good, the manager prospers; but if the sponsor underperforms for too long, he or she doesn't have to go down with the ship. Instead, many managers choose to simply liquidate the fund and start a fresh one, letting his limited partners suffer the losses. Because of this flawed design, the most significant risk factor in a hedge fund is often the honesty and character of the general partner. In a hedge fund structure, the limited partners most likely put all their investment into the fund up front. From then on, the general partner has total control, including the final say in whether any investor can withdraw from the fund. As if that weren't already pulling enough strings, the general partner can also *withdraw* cash with little oversight. This is a structure practically designed to be exploited, and as a result, nearly every week brings reports of yet another hedge fund manager who has mismanaged, borrowed, or just plain stolen the cash of his fund and investors. This kind of investment is hardly what you might expect from any firm you've entrusted with your assets, but it is commonplace among Wall Street's major players.

Private equity is another alternative investment Wall Street sometimes offers. Like a hedge fund manager, the private equity sponsor earns an annual fee and a percent of profits. Unlike a hedge fund, though, the private equity investor can earn much more in terms of consulting fees and deal fees. The catch is that Wall Street firms do not have access to the outstanding managers. Many top-tier private equity sponsors work directly with institutional buyers, choosing not to deal with Wall Street or individual investors. As a result, the private equity options offered by Wall Street are often second-tier funds or are investments run by the "B team" managers of the large well-recognized firms.

WALL STREET IS ALL ABOUT THE QUICK BUCK

Finally, the culture of a Wall Street firm is sales, sales, sales. When an idea is hot, Wall Street quickly creates new products to capture investors' imaginations—whether those products are prudent in the long term or not. A current example is the proliferation of exchange-traded funds (ETFs). These funds are designed with instant liquidity in mind, but Wall Street is creating ETFs with underlying securities that are illiquid in the best of markets—and can freeze in a market crisis. What will Wall Street do when an ETF sponsor cannot honor its liquidity promise? Sadly, it won't matter to the big institutions that are supposed to be looking out for their investors' best interests. By then, the brokers will have moved enough of the product to make their profit, and they'll have shifted their focus to the next in an endless supply of hot products their unsuspecting investors will line up to buy—all the while mistakenly believing that a big-named Wall Street firm has their financial wellness in mind.

LIE #5

THE WALL STREET MODEL IS INVESTING'S GOLD STANDARD

←1-9
WALL ST

Whether you sold a business, retired from a successful career, or inherited a large sum of money, you're probably focused on preserving your wealth and living off the nest egg you worked hard to create. All too often, the partners here at Oxbow talk with people in similar financial circumstances who have already been misguided by Wall Street advisors. These investors did not fully understand their needs and were too easily misled by the Wall Street party line. They were told to invest nearly all their assets in the markets and to diversify within those parameters. That advice is the Wall Street model in a nutshell—and it is anything but a gold standard. Experienced, ethical, proactive financial advisors know they have a responsibility first to preserve their investors' capital and second to grow it in the short and long term. The all-in mentality Wall Street pushes on its investors can have ruinous results.

The typical Wall Street investment advisor will tell you that you need to diversify your risk. You need X percent in stocks and Y percent in bonds, based on your age and risk tolerance. This advisor is usually focused on balancing your riskier growth-oriented investments (stocks) with lower-risk investments (typically bonds). He or she will undoubtedly try to convince you that the magic formula balances risk and return, maybe even running a Monte Carlo simulation or something similar. The problem with those simulations is that they're full of assumptions—such as the one that says the market always goes up. With this investment model in mind, a Wall Street money manager will chop up your equity and allocate you to US, non-US, value, growth, emerging markets, sector-specific managers, and other investments. Some managers may even get fancy and proclaim that you need some alternative investment exposure. Almost unanimously, they will advise you to invest the vast majority of your net worth in the markets.

In our experience here at Oxbow—based on decades of conscientious financial advising for well-off investors around the country—Wall Street flat out has this wrong. Their model does not consider the big picture of your financial future. Just look at what happened to a portfolio of 50 percent bonds and 50 percent stocks—a portfolio that most on Wall Street would consider to be fairly conservative—during the financial crisis of 2008. From peak to trough, stocks lost more than 50 percent while the bonds earned about 10 percent, resulting in more than a -20 percent overall loss. That doesn't seem like a conservative approach does it?

By contrast, here's the Oxbow model. If you have a significant amount of wealth, then it is imprudent to put it all at risk in the markets. It is our belief that you should keep 25 percent to 30 percent on the sidelines. At some point, you will get a fat pitch—and that will be the time to potentially put some of it to work. With the portion of your assets that you allocate for investing, you should move slowly, err on the side of caution, and focus on generating cash flow. If you are like most of our investors, you are *not* in the business of getting rich quick. You are already financially secure—a security you earned through hard work, wise investments, *calculated* risks, and smart choices. Your focus should be on maintaining what you have built and creating enough cash flow from your portfolio to maintain your lifestyle for all of your years. In essence, this is making your investments provide for you much like your business or career previously did.

The Oxbow investment model is one in which we view the investment universe in two categories: *base capital* and *investment capital*. Base capital is put in place for capital preservation and used to create a cash flow stream you can live on. For some, this may be

100 percent of assets; for others, it may be 50 percent or less. This part of a portfolio should be highly liquid. One portion should be in high-quality bonds and the other portion in cash-flowing securities. The mix of the two is different for each individual, based on risk profile and cash flow needs. Only after this part of the portfolio is in place should someone with a substantial nest egg begin to think about investment capital, including higher risk investments like stocks, real estate, private companies, oil and gas, etc. Not everyone needs or will want to allocate funds to investment capital, but it is essential that each investor have base capital—and the cash flow it provides—in place.

As you can see, the Oxbow investment model is based on a completely different set of priorities and objectives from the Wall Street model. Before you entrust the proceeds of your business, your inheritance, or your life's savings to any advisor, take the time to ask yourself what kind of investment model is consistent with the way you've lived your life, built your business, and managed your own affairs. Unless you're a gambler at heart, you may well find that the Oxbow principles are a far better reflection of what matters to you than the go-for-broke Wall Street mentality that has gotten so many investors before you into deep and lasting financial trouble.

CONCLUSION

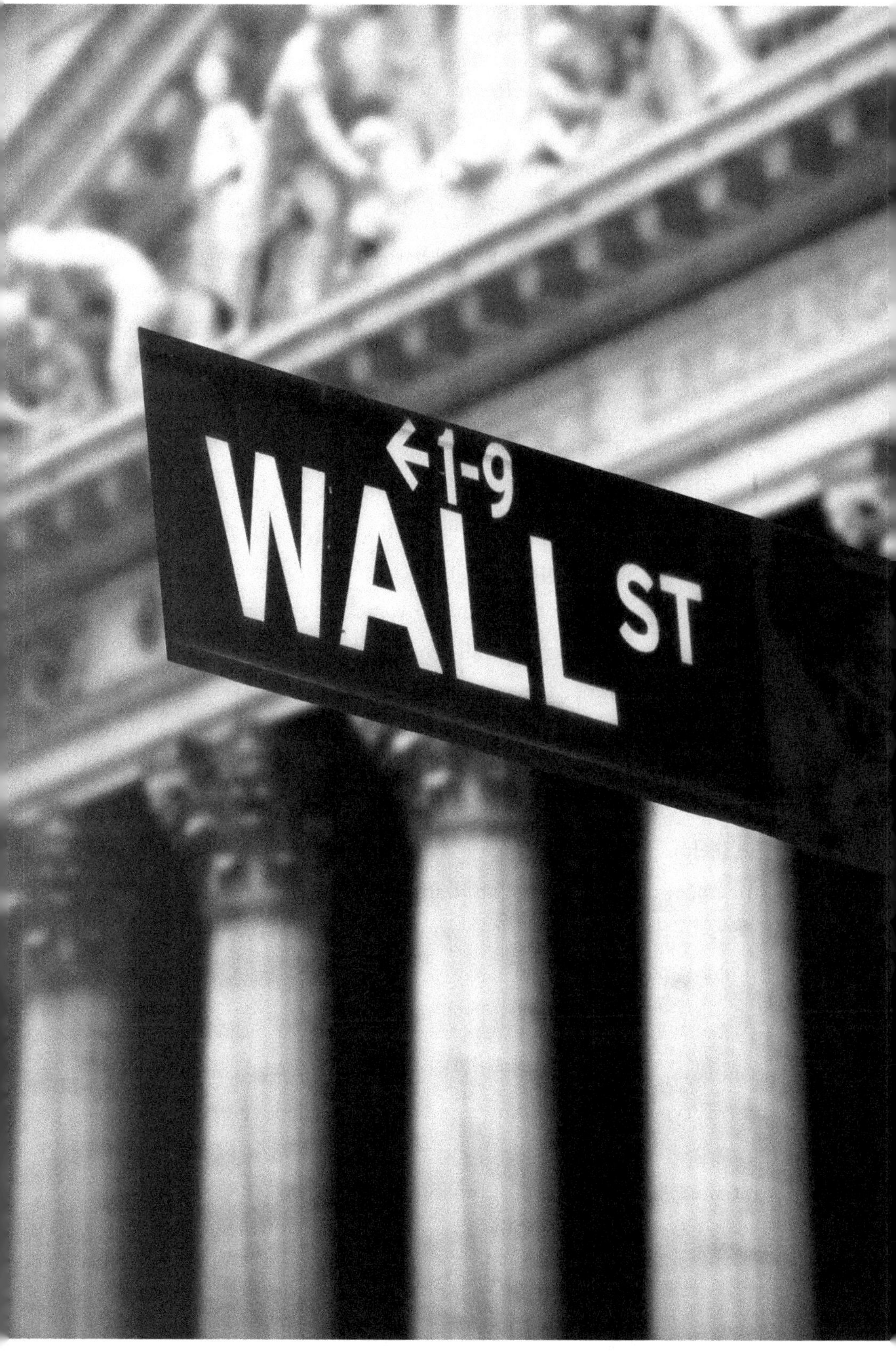
←1-9
WALL ST

Year after year, decade after decade, the Wall Street brokerage industry has repeatedly been exposed for the self-serving and unreliable institution it has become. But some of the most insidious facts of its existence are still kept largely hidden from the public. The most glaring of these secrets may be the size and scope of the efforts Wall Street makes through political campaign donations and lobbying to ensure it remains largely unregulated. Part and parcel with this is its dedication to keeping the lines between the brokerage industry and the legitimate profession of financial advising as blurred and indistinguishable to the investing public as possible. To that end, the financial services industry has been far and away the biggest contributor to candidates in every recent election cycle. And if you look at the largest contributing banks, Wall Street predominates, with almost *all* of the top contributors coming from the brokerage side of the industry. This trend toward Wall Street throwing its resources behind its continued competitive edge extends to lobbying as well. During the debate over Dodd-Frank legislation in 2012, for example, Wall Street lobbyists intent on preventing finance reform outnumbered consumer protection group lobbyists by a margin of *twenty to one.* And if those facts aren't enough to stack the odds for the brokerage industry, consider the fact that many of the top leaders and decision makers in the federal financial posts are in fact former Wall Street insiders.

As an investor who's worked all your life to build a business, accumulate assets, and plan a future that is free of financial worry, you deserve to know just how powerful and deceptive the brokerage industry can be. Most of us intuitively know that Wall Street can't be trusted, but we hope these chapters have helped to clarify exactly why.

If you are on the verge of making investment decisions that will have a long-term impact on your financial future, we urge you to be guarded against the aggressive and predatory sales tactics Wall Street will likely send your way. As you weigh your options, ask yourself in each case if the institution you're considering entrusting with the assets you've accumulated through decades of hard work and prudent choices really has your best interests at heart. If the answer is no, keep looking. You can find a better steward of your wealth. There are trusted and stalwart investment groups like the management at Oxbow Advisors out there, and we are diligently working to protect and grow our investors' money—all the while giving the chicanery and shadowy practices of Wall Street's notorious brokerage houses a wide berth.

ABOUT THE AUTHORS

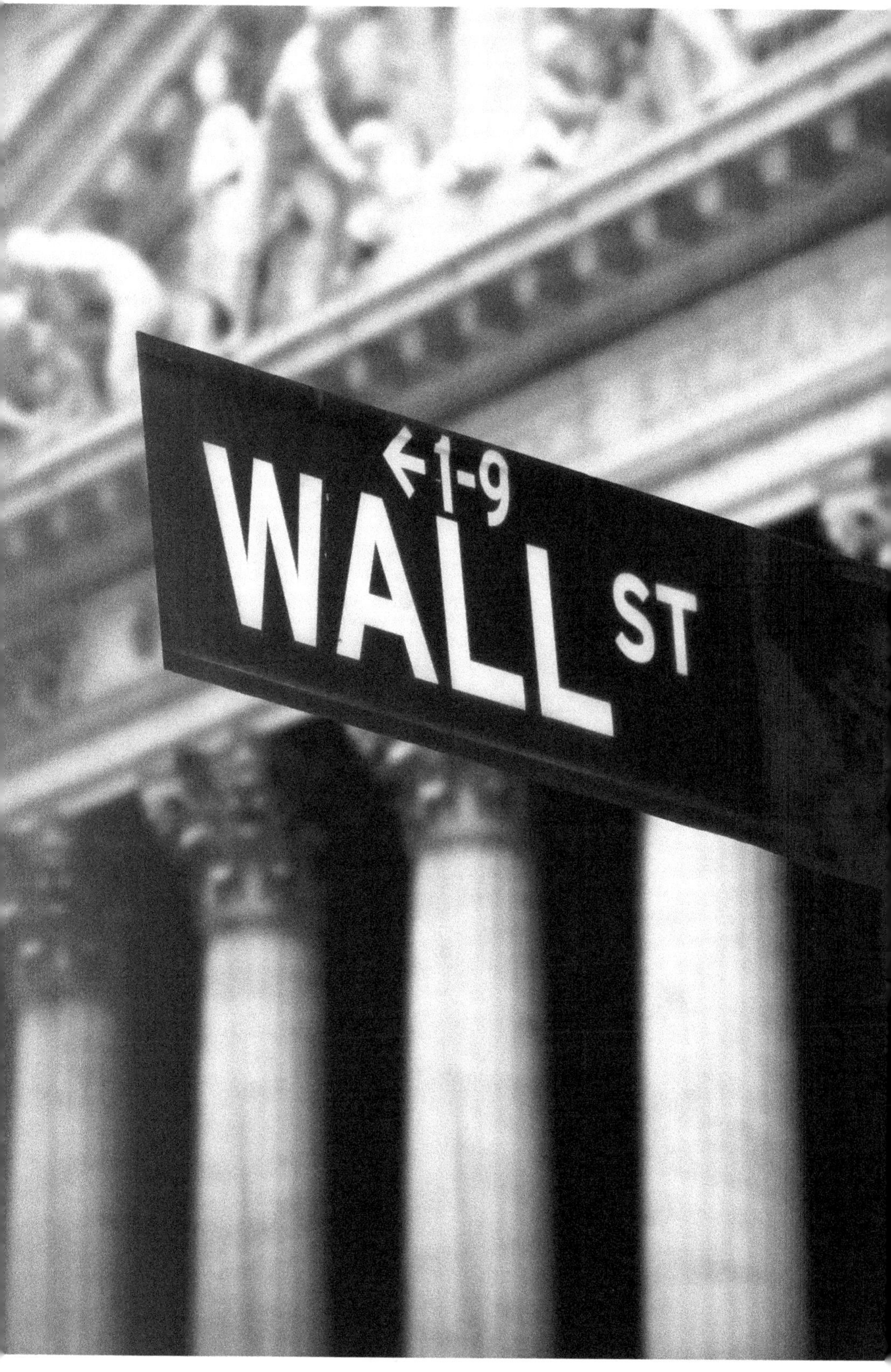
←1-9
WALL ST

J. TED OAKLEY, founder and managing partner of Oxbow Advisors, began his career in the investment industry in 1975. The "Oxbow Principles" and the firm's proprietary investment strategies are founded on the unique perspective he has gained during his decades-long tenure advising high-net-worth investors. Ted's investment advice provides principled guidance to investors from more than half the states in America. He frequently counsels former business owners on protecting and wisely investing their newly liquid wealth. Ted is the author of four other books:

- *You Sold Your Company*
- *$20 Million and Broke*
- *Rich Kids, Poor Kids: The Failure of Traditional Estate Planning*
- *Crazy Time: Surviving the First 12 Months after Selling Your Company Without Losing Your Fortune—or Your Mind.*

ABOUT THE AUTHORS

PAT SWANSON, CFA, partner and director of research at Oxbow, began his investment career in 1984. Prior to joining Oxbow, Pat had been with King Investment Advisors, Inc. (KING) for twenty-one years. He is a graduate of the United States Air Force Academy with a BS in economics and an MBA from Pepperdine University. Pat was managing director and chief compliance officer for KING, as well as a member of the firm's investment advisory group. Pat is a member of Oxbow's investment committee.

TREY CRAIN, partner and portfolio manager, has an economics degree from Rice University and joined Oxbow in 2011. Trey is a member of the firm's investment committee, and he works with business owners across the US who have recently sold their companies.

Printed in the USA
CPSIA information can be obtained
at www.ICGtesting.com
JSHW011321070724
65942JS00007B/56

9 781599 327518